Slow Cooke:
Simple and Delicious Cˑ _ _ _ _ _ _ _ _ _ _ _ _ _ _
for Busy People on a Budget

by **Alissa Noel Grey**
Text copyright(c)2017 Alissa Noel Grey

Table Of Contents

Delicious Crock-Pot Meals to Please Everyone

We just love the cozy feeling of sitting down with our family to a home-cooked dinner! But we also live in an age when we are constantly on the move and putting a home-cooked meal on the table during a busy weeknight looks like an impossible endeavor. As a busy mom, I love using my crock pot. In my new cookbook I have gathered the very best of my slow cooker family recipes for evening meals, inspired by my Mediterranean origins, and prepared using local and easy to find ingredients.

Slow cookers save time, money and energy, and are generally a budget-friendly way to prepare food. All my slow cooker recipes have a few things in common – they are healthy, they are budget-friendly, and they can be prepared even by an inexperienced cook.

Slow cooker recipes are such a time saver for busy mums. All you need to do is cut up your favorite vegetables, meats and legumes, throw them together with your favorite spices in the slow cooker and you will have a quick weeknight supper or a delicious weekend dinner-it doesn't get any easier than that! Set and forget at the beginning of the day and come home to a delicious healthy dinner the whole family will love!.

Healthy Italian Chicken Soup

Serves: 4

Prep time: 5 min

Cooking time: 5-7 hours

Ingredients:

3 chicken breasts

1 carrot, chopped

1 small zucchini, peeled and chopped

1 celery stalk, chopped

1 small onion, chopped

2 garlic cloves

1 bay leaf

4 cups water

6-7 black olives, pitted and halved

1/2 tsp salt

1 tsp dried basil

2 tbsp extra virgin olive oil

black pepper, to taste

fresh parsley, to serve

lemon juice, to serve

Directions:

In a skillet, gently sauté the onion and garlic in olive oil, for 2-3 minutes, or until transparent. Add them together with all other ingredients to the slow cooker.

Cook on low for 5-7 hours, or on high for 3 1/2.

Remove chicken from the slow cooker and set aside to cool. Shred it and return it back to the crock pot. Serve with lemon juice and sprinkled with parsley.

Chicken and Butternut Squash Soup

Serves: 4

Prep time: 2-3 min

Cooking time: 5-7 hours

Ingredients:

3 boneless chicken thighs, diced

1/2 onion, chopped

6-7 white mushrooms, chopped

1 small zucchini, peeled and diced

1 cup butternut squash, diced

1 tbsp tomato paste

4 cups water

1/4 tsp cumin

1 tbsp paprika

3 tbsp extra virgin olive oil

Directions:

In a skillet, gently sauté the onion and chicken in olive oil for 2-3 minutes. Stir in cumin and paprika. Add this mixture together with all other ingredients to the slow cooker. Season with salt and black pepper to taste.

Cook on low for 5-7 hours, or on high for 3 1/2.

Old-Fashioned Chicken Soup

Serves: 4

Prep time: 2 min

Cooking time: 5-6 hours

Ingredients:

3 boneless chicken tights, diced

1 small onion, chopped

3 garlic cloves

1 potato, peeled and diced

1 large carrot, chopped

1 red bell pepper, chopped

1 celery stalk, chopped

1/2 cup vermicelli

1 bay leaf

1 tsp salt

1/2 cup fresh parsley leaves, finely cut

black pepper, to taste

Directions:

Place the chicken, bay leaf, carrot, onion, tomatoes, potato and salt into slow cooker with 4 cups of cold water.

Cook on low for 5-6 hours, or on high for 4.

Add in vermicelli, season with salt and pepper, add in parsley, cover, and cook on low 20 minutes. Serve with lemon juice or Greek yogurt.

Slow Cooked Chicken and Bean Soup

Serves: 4

Prep time: 2 min

Cooking time: 5-6 hours

Ingredients:

3 boneless chicken tights, chopped

1 small onion, chopped

3 garlic cloves

1 can diced tomatoes

1 large carrot, chopped

1 can black beans, drained and rinsed

3 cups chicken broth

1 bay leaf

1/2 tsp cumin

1 tsp salt

1/2 cup fresh parsley leaves, finely cut

black pepper, to taste

Directions:

Combine all ingredients in slow cooker.

Cover and cook on low for 5-6 hours, or on high for 4.

Creamy Chicken Soup

Serves: 4

Prep time: 2 min

Cooking time: 5-6 hours

Ingredients:

4 chicken breasts

1 carrot, chopped

1 cup zucchini, peeled and chopped

2 cups cauliflower, broken into florets

1 celery rib, chopped

1 small onion, chopped

4 cups water

1/2 tsp salt

black pepper, to taste

Directions:

Place chicken breasts, onion, carrot, celery, cauliflower and zucchini in slow cooker. Add in salt, black pepper and 4 cups of water. Stir to combine.

Cook on low for 5-6 hours, or on high for 4 then remove chicken from the crock pot and let it cool slightly.

Blend soup until completely smooth. Shred or dice the chicken meat, return it back to the crock pot, stir, and serve.

Broccoli and Chicken Soup

Serves: 4

Prep time: 5 min

Cooking time: 5-6 hours

Ingredients:

4 boneless chicken thighs, diced

1 small carrot, chopped

1 broccoli head, broken into florets

1 garlic clove, chopped

1 small onion, chopped

4 cups water

3 tbsp extra virgin olive oil

1/2 tsp salt

black pepper, to taste

Directions:

In a skillet, heat olive oil and gently sauté broccoli for 2-3 minutes, stirring occasionally. Add in onion, carrot, chicken and cook, stirring, for 2-3 minutes.

Add this mixture together with all other ingredients to the slow cooker. Stir to combine.

Cook on low for 5-6 hours, or on high for 4.

In a blender or food processor, blend soup until completely smooth. Serve and enjoy!

Turkey and Ricotta Meatball Soup

Serves: 4-5

Prep time: 5 min

Cooking time: 5-7 hours

Ingredients:

1 lb ground turkey meat

1 egg, lightly whisked

1 cup whole milk ricotta

1 cup grated Parmesan cheese

4 tbsp flour

1/2 onion, finely cut

4 cups chicken broth

2 cups baby spinach leaves

1 tsp dried thyme leaves

½ tsp black pepper

Directions:

Place ground turkey meat, Ricotta, Parmesan, egg and black pepper. Combine well with hands and roll teaspoonfuls of the mixture into balls. Place flour in a shallow bowl and roll each meatball in the flour then set aside on a large plate.

Add meatballs and all ingredients to slow cooker.

Cook on low for 5-7 hours, or on high for 4-5.

Add baby spinach and cook for 20 more minutes on high.

Italian Beef and Vegetable Soup

Serves: 4-5

Prep time: 5 min

Cooking time: 6-7 hours

Ingredients:

2 slices bacon, chopped

1 lb lean ground beef

1 carrot, chopped

2 cloves garlic, finely chopped

1 small onion, chopped

1 celery stalk, chopped

1 bay leaf

1 tsp dried basil

1 cup canned tomatoes, diced and drained

4 cups beef broth

1/2 cup canned chickpeas

½ cup vermicelli

Directions:

In a skillet, cook bacon and ground beef until well done, breaking up the beef as it cooks. Drain off the fat and add in onion, garlic, carrot and celery. Cook for 3-4 minutes until fragrant.

Transfer to slow cooker and stir in the bay leaf, basil, tomatoes and beef broth. Add in chickpeas.

Cook on low for 6-7 hours, or on high for 4-5.

Add vermicelli, stir, and cook on high for 20 minutes.

Barley Beef Soup

Serves: 4-5

Prep time: 6-7 min

Cooking time: 6-7 hours

Ingredients:

12 oz beef stew meat, cut into 1 inch cubes

1 medium leek, chopped

2 garlic cloves, chopped

2 bay leaves

1 can tomatoes (15 oz), diced and drained

1/2 cup barley

1 cup frozen mixed vegetables

4 cups beef broth

2 tbsp extra virgin olive oil

1 tsp paprika

Directions:

Heat oil in a skillet over medium-high heat. Sauté beef until well browned. Add in leeks and garlic and sauté until fragrant.

Transfer to slow cooker. Add paprika, beef broth and bay leaves; season with salt and pepper.

Cook on low for 6-7 hours, or on high for 4.

Stir in frozen vegetables, tomatoes, and barley. Cook on high for 2 hours. Discard bay leaves and serve.

Hearty Meatball Soup

Serves: 4-5

Prep time: 6-7 min

Cooking time: 5-6 hours

Ingredients:

1 lb lean ground beef

1 egg, lightly whisked

1/2 onion, chopped

2 garlic cloves, chopped

1 tomato, diced

2 potatoes, diced

1/2 red bell pepper, chopped

4 cups water

4 tbsp flour

1 cup vermicelli, broken into pieces

½ bunch of parsley, finely cut

3 tbsp extra virgin olive oil

½ tsp black pepper

1 tsp paprika

1 tsp salt

Directions:

Place ground meat, egg, black pepper and salt in a bowl. Combine well with hands and roll teaspoonfuls of the mixture into balls. Place flour in a shallow bowl and roll each meatball in the flour then set aside on a large plate.

in a skillet, heat olive oil and gently sauté onion and garlic until transparent.

Transfer to slow cooker, add in water, meatballs, carrot, pepper, tomato and potatoes.

Cook on low for 6-7 hours, or on high for 4-5.

Add parsley and vermicelli and cook for 20 more minutes on high. Serve with a dollop of yogurt on top.

Spiced Beet and Carrot Soup

Serves: 4-5

Prep time: 5 min

Cooking time: 5-6 hours

Ingredients:

3 beets, washed and peeled

2 carrots, peeled and chopped

1 small onion, chopped

1 garlic clove, chopped

3 cups vegetable broth

1 cup water

2 tbsp extra virgin olive oil

1 tsp grated ginger

1 tsp grated orange peel

Directions:

Heat olive oil in a skillet. Add the onion and sauté over low heat for 3-4 minutes or until translucent. Add the garlic, beets, carrots, ginger and orange rind.

Transfer this mixture to slow cooker and add water and vegetable broth.

Cook on low for 5-6 hours, or on high for 3 1/2.

Cool slightly and blend soup in batches until smooth. Season with salt and pepper and serve.

Mushroom and Kale Soup

Serves: 4-5

Prep time: 2 min

Cooking time: 5-6 hours

Ingredients:

1 onion, chopped

1 carrot, chopped

1 zucchini, peeled and diced

1 potato, peeled and diced

10 white mushrooms, chopped

1 bunch kale (10 oz), stemmed and coarsely chopped

3 cups vegetable broth

salt and black pepper, to taste

Directions:

Combine all ingredients except the kale in the slow cooker.

Cover and cook on low for 5-6 hours or on high for 4 hours.

Stir in the kale and cook for 20 more minutes on high.

Pumpkin and Bell Pepper Soup

Serves: 4-5

Prep time: 2 min

Cooking time: 5-6 hours

Ingredients:

1/2 small onion, chopped

3 cups pumpkin cubes

2 red bell peppers, chopped

1 carrot, chopped

3 cups vegetable broth

3 tbsp extra virgin olive oil

1/2 tsp cumin

salt and black pepper, to taste

Combine all ingredients in the slow cooker.

Cover and cook on low for 5-6 hours or on high for 4 hours.

Season with salt and pepper, blend in batches, and serve.

Leek, Pea and Potato Soup

Serves: 4-5

Prep time: 2 min

Cooking time: 5-6 hours

Ingredients:

3 potatoes, peeled and diced

2 leeks, finely chopped

1 cup frozen peas

4 cups water

lemon juice, to taste

Directions:

Combine all ingredients in the slow cooker.

Cover and cook on low for 5-6 hours or on high for 4 hours.

Add lemon juice, to taste, and serve.

Minted Pea and Nettle Soup

Serves: 4

Prep time: 5 min

Cooking time: 5-6 hours

Ingredients:

1 onion, chopped

3-4 garlic cloves, chopped

4 cups vegetable broth

2 tbsp dried mint leaves

1 16 oz bag frozen green peas

about 20 nettle tops

fresh dill, finely chopped, to serve

Directions:

Heat oil in a large saucepan over medium-high heat and sauté onion and garlic for 3-4 minutes.

Combine all ingredients in the slow cooker.

Cover and cook on low for 5-6 hours or on high for 4 hours.

Set aside to cool slightly, then blend in batches, until smooth. Season with salt and pepper. Serve sprinkled with fresh dill.

Easy Beef Crock Pot

Serves 4

Prep time: 5 min

Cooking time: 7-9 hours

Ingredients:

2 lbs beef, cubed

3-4 leeks, finely cut

1 celery rib, finely cut

10 white button mushrooms, sliced

1 cup milk

1 tsp dried thyme

1 tsp salt

1/2 tsp black pepper

2 tbsp extra virgin olive oil

Directions:

Spray the slow cooker with non stick spray.

In a skillet, brown the beef for 1-2 minutes or until sealed.

Combine all ingredients into the slow cooker, cover, and cook on low for 7-9 hours.

Hearty Meatball Stew

Serves: 6

Prep time: 5 min

Cooking time: 7-9 hours

Ingredients:

for the meatballs:

2 lbs ground beef

1 onion, finely copped

1/3 cup parsley leaves, finely chopped

for the sauce:

1/2 small onion, chopped

1 carrot, chopped

1 red pepper, cut

1 zucchini, peeled and cut

1/2 eggplant, peeled and diced

2 garlic cloves, chopped

4 white mushrooms, sliced

1 can tomatoes, diced, undrained

1/2 cup chicken broth

1/2 cup parsley leaves, to serve

salt and black pepper, to taste

Directions:

Combine ground beef, onion, parsley, salt and pepper in a bowl. Roll tablespoonfuls of beef mixture into balls and set aside on plate.

Combine all ingredients into the slow cooker, cover, and cook on low for 7-9 hours.

Sprinkle with parsley and serve.

Slow Cooked Pot Roast

Serves 6

Prep time: 5 min

Cooking time: 9-11 hours

Ingredients:

2 lb pot roast

4 garlic cloves, crushed

2 onions, sliced

6 carrots, quartered

4 celery ribs, cut into thick pieces

4 tbsp tomato paste

1 cup chicken broth

1 tbsp finely chopped rosemary

1/4 tsp black pepper

1 tbsp dried basil

1 tbsp dried oregano

Directions:

Spray the slow cooker with non stick spray.

Sprinkle salt, black pepper, basil, rosemary and oregano over the roast and place in the slow cooker.

In a bowl, combine the tomato paste and chicken broth. Pour this mixture over the meat. Arrange vegetables around the meat.

Cover and cook on low 9-11 hours.

Slow Cooked Beef with Quince, Parsnips and Carrots

Serves 6

Prep time: 5 min

Cooking time: 9-11 hours

Ingredients:

2-3 lb roast beef round

4 parsnips, peeled, quartered lengthwise

6 carrots, quartered lengthwise

2 quinces, peeled, cored and cubed

1 cup beef or chicken broth

2 tbsp apple puree

1 tbsp Dijon mustard

3 tbsp extra virgin olive oil

black pepper and salt, to taste

Directions:

Spray the slow cooker with non stick spray.

Sprinkle salt and black pepper over the roast and place in the slow cooker.

In a bowl, whisk together beef broth, apple puree and mustard until smooth. Pour this mixture over the meat. Arrange parsnips, carrots and quinces around the meat.

Cover and cook on low 9-11 hours.

Beef and Onion Crock Pot

Serves 6

Prep time: 2 min

Cooking time: 7-9 hours

Ingredients:

2 lbs lean beef, cut in cubes

2 lbs shallots, peeled

2-3 garlic cloves, peeled, whole

3 tbsp tomato paste, dissolved in 1/2 cup water

2 cups chicken broth

2 bay leaves

4 tbsp red wine vinegar

1 tsp salt

Directions:

Combine all ingredients in crock pot. Cover and cook on low for 7-9 hours.

Beef and Green Pea Crock Pot

Serves 6

Prep time: 2 min

Cooking time: 7-9 hours

Ingredients:

2 lbs stewing beef

2 bags frozen peas

1 onion, chopped

2 carrots, chopped

3-4 garlic cloves, cut

2 cups chicken broth

1 tsp salt

1 tbsp paprika

1/2 cup fresh dill, finely chopped

1 cup yogurt, to serve

Directions:

Combine all ingredients in crock pot.

Cover and cook on low for 7-9 hours. Serve sprinkled with dill and a dollop of yogurt.

Slow Cooked Mediterranean Beef

Serves 6

Prep time: 5 min

Cooking time: 7-9 hours

Ingredients:

2 lbs lean steak, cut into large pieces

2 onions, sliced

2-3 garlic cloves, whole

1 green pepper, cut

1/2 bag frozen green beans

1/2 bag frozen green peas

1/2 bag frozen okra

1 zucchini, peeled and cut

1 small eggplant, peeled and diced

1 tomato, diced

2 tbsp tomato paste or purée

1 cup chicken broth

1 tsp dried oregano

salt and black pepper, to taste

Directions:

Combine all ingredients in crock pot.

Cover and cook on low for 7-9 hours.

Slow Cooked Beef with Sweet Potatoes

Serves: 4-5

Serves 6

Prep time: 5 min

Cooking time: 7-9 hours

Ingredients:

2 lbs stewing beef

2 ripe tomatoes, peeled and sliced

1 lb sweet potatoes, peeled and cut into slices

1 onion, finely chopped

½ tsp turmeric

½ tsp black pepper

1/2 tsp paprika

1/4 tsp ground ginger

½ tsp cumin

1 bunch of fresh cilantro

1 bunch of fresh parsley

Directions:

Place beef in slow cooker; top with sweet potatoes, tomatoes and onion.

Add in turmeric, salt, black pepper and all remaining spices. Tie the parsley and cilantro together into a bouquet and place on top of the beef.

Cover and cook on low for 7-9 hours.

Remove the parsley and cilantro bouquet and serve.

Slow Cooked Ground Beef and Cabbage

Serves: 4-5

Prep time: 5 min

Cooking time: 5-6 hours

Ingredients:

1 lb ground beef

1/2 cabbage, shredded

1/2 onion, chopped

2 leeks, white part only, chopped

1 tomato, diced

1/3 cup chicken broth

1 tbsp paprika

1/2 tsp cumin

½ tsp black pepper

4 tbsp extra virgin olive oil

salt, to taste

Directions:

In a deep saucepan, sauté the onion and leeks in olive oil until tender. Add in the ground beef, tomato, paprika, cumin, salt and black pepper and sauté for 2-3 minutes more, stirring.

Add the cooked ground beef, shredded cabbage, and chicken broth to a slow cooker. Stir to combine, cover, and cook on low for 5-6 hours.

Slow Cooked Beef and Chickpea Couscous

Serves 5-6

Prep time: 2 min

Cooking time: 10 hours

Ingredients:

2 lbs stewing beef

1 onion, cut

1 can chickpeas, drained

2 carrots, cut

1/2 cup green peas

1/2 cup black olives, pitted

3 tbsp tomato paste

2 cups water

1 small zucchini, peeled and cut

1 cup frozen green beans

3 potatoes, peeled and cut

1 tsp cumin

1 tsp paprika

a small bunch of fresh parsley

Directions:

Place beef, onion, chickpeas, green peas, carrot, olives, tomato paste, cumin, paprika and water in slow cooker. Tie the parsley into a bouquet and place it on top. Cover and cook on low for 9 hours.

Add green beans, potatoes and zucchini, season with salt and pepper to taste, increase heat setting to high and cook for 1 hour more. In the end discard the parsley bouquet.

Serve over cooked couscous with meat and vegetables on top and stew sauce in a separate bowl.

Slow Cooked Beef and Barley Stew

Serves 5-6

Prep time: 6-7 min

Cooking time: 6-8 hours

Ingredients:

2 lbs stewing beef

1 onion, cut

2 carrots, cut

1 celery rib, chopped

1 cup barley

4 cups beef broth

1 tbsp tomato paste

1 bay leaf

1 tsp paprika

2 tbsp olive oil

Directions:

In a skillet over medium high heat add olive oil and brown beef in small batches. Place in slow cooker.

Add in onions, carrots, celery and beef broth. Stir in paprika, tomato paste and barley. Add the bay leaf.

Cover and cook on low for 6-8 hours.

Slow Cooked Ground Beef and Cauliflower Stew

Serves: 4-5

Prep time: 5 min

Cooking time: 5-6 hours

Ingredients:

1 lb ground beef

1 medium head cauliflower, cut into florets

1/2 onion, chopped

1 tomato, diced

1/2 cup chicken broth

1/2 cup heavy cream

1 tbsp paprika

½ tsp black pepper

2 tbsp extra virgin olive oil

salt, to taste

Directions:

In a deep saucepan, sauté the onion in olive oil until transparent. Add in the ground beef and sauté for 2-3 minutes more, stirring.

Add the cooked ground beef, cauliflower florets, tomato, paprika, cream and chicken broth to a slow cooker. Season with black pepper and salt and stir to combine.

Cover, and cook on low for 5-6 hours.

Blue Cheese and Mushroom Chicken

Serves 4

Prep time: 5 min

Cooking time: 5-6 hours

Ingredients:

4 chicken breast halves

5-6 white button mushrooms, chopped

1/2 cup mushroom soup

1/2 cup crumbled blue cheese

1/2 cup sour cream

salt and black pepper, to taste

1/2 cup parsley, finely cut

Directions:

Spray the slow cooker with non stick spray. Place all ingredients into it, turn chicken to coat.

Cover and cook on low for 5-6 hours. Sprinkle with parsley and serve.

Slow Cooker Paprika Chicken

Serves 4

Prep time: 2 min

Cooking time: 5-6 hours

Ingredients:

8 chicken drumsticks or 4 breast halves

1 onion, chopped

3 slices bacon, finely chopped

1 large red pepper, chopped

1 large green pepper, chopped

2-3 garlic cloves, finely chopped

1 tbsp paprika

1/2 can crushed tomatoes

11/2 cup chicken broth

1/3 cup medium-grain white rice

1 tbsp sour cream

1 cup fresh parsley, finely cut, to serve

Directions:

Combine all ingredients in slow cooker. Cover and cook on low for 5-6 hours.

One-Pot Chicken and Rainbow Vegetables

Serves 4-5

Prep time: 2 min

Cooking time: 5-6 hours

Ingredients:

2 lbs chicken breast tenderloins

1 bunch fresh asparagus, trimmed of tough ends, chopped into matchsticks

2 large carrots cut into matchsticks

1 yellow capsicum cut into matchsticks

1 cup grape tomatoes, halved

2 tbsp honey

¼ cup orange juice

3 tbsp balsamic vinegar

½ tsp dried basil

½ tsp dried oregano

salt and freshly ground black pepper, to taste

Directions:

Mix together orange juice, balsamic vinegar, honey, basil and oregano in a mixing bowl.

Spray the slow cooker with non stick spray. Place chicken in slow cooker. Add in asparagus, peppers, carrots and tomatoes and season with salt and pepper to taste.

Add prepared honey mixture. Cover and cook on low for 5-6 hours.

Cumin Chicken with Black Beans

Serves 4

Prep time: 2 min

Cooking time: 5-6 hours

Ingredients:

4 chicken breast halves, diced

1 tsp cumin

¼ tsp cayenne pepper

2 tbsp extra virgin olive oil

1 red onion, finely cut

3 cups cooked black beans, rinsed and drained

1 cup frozen corn, thawed

1 cup cherry tomatoes, halved

1/3 cup cilantro, finely cut

salt and black pepper, to taste

Directions:

Combine the cumin with the cayenne and rub over the chicken.

Spray the slow cooker with non stick spray. Place chicken in slow cooker. Add in onion, the beans, corn, and tomatoes. Stir in the cilantro and season to taste with salt and black pepper.

Cover and cook on low heat for 5-6 hours.

Chicken Cutlets With Tomato Sauté

Serves 4

Prep time: 2 min

Cooking time: 5-6 hours

Ingredients:

2 lbs chicken cutlet

2 cups cherry tomatoes

1/3 cup dry white wine

1 cup spring onions, finely cut

3 tbsp fresh tarragon leaves, chopped

1 tsp garlic powder

1 tsp paprika

salt and pepper, to taste

Directions:

Season the chicken with salt, pepper paprika and garlic.

Spray the slow cooker with non stick spray. Place chicken in slow cooker. Top with the tomatoes and spring onions and add in the wine.

Cover and cook on low heat for 5-6 hours.

Slow Cooked Pesto Chicken

Serves 4

Prep time: 2 min

Cooking time: 5-6 hours

Ingredients:

5-6 chicken breast halves

1 small jar pesto sauce

1 cup sour cream

Directions:

Spray the slow cooker with non stick spray.

Place all ingredients into slow cooker and turn chicken to coat well.

Cook on low for 5-6 hours.

Mediterranean Chicken Stew

Serves: 4

Prep time: 2 min

Cooking time: 5-6 hours

Ingredients:

4 chicken breasts

1 onion, chopped

1 small zucchini, peeled and chopped

1 red bell pepper, chopped

1 cup tomato sauce

1 cup assorted olives, pitted

1 tsp dried basil

1/2 cup fresh parsley, finely chopped

Directions:

Spray the slow cooker with non stick spray.

Place the chicken breasts in it and cover with the onion, bell pepper, zucchini, tomato sauce, olives, basil, salt and pepper.

Cover and cook on low heat for 5-6 hours. Sprinkle with fresh parsley and serve.

Slow Cooked Chicken and Onion

Serves: 4

Prep time: 2 min

Cooking time: 5-6 hours

Ingredients:

4 chicken breasts

6-7 large onions, sliced

1 cup black olives, pitted

1 bay leaf

1 tsp thyme

1 tsp sugar

salt and black pepper, to taste

Directions:

Spray the slow cooker with non stick spray.

Place the chicken breasts in the slow cooker and cover with the sliced onion and olives. Add in the thyme, bay leaf and sugar. Season with salt and pepper to taste.

Cover and cook on low heat for 4-5 hours. Discard the bay leaf and serve.

Chicken Drumsticks with Broccoli and Sweet Potatoes

Serves: 4

Prep time: 5 min

Cooking time: 5-6 hours

Ingredients:

8 chicken drumsticks

1 head broccoli, cut into florets

1 leek, sliced

1 garlic clove, crushed

1 sweet potato, peeled and cubed

1 carrot, cut

1 tsp dried rosemary

3 tbsp olive oil

1 tsp dried oregano

salt and black pepper, to taste

Directions:

Heat the olive oil in a casserole over medium heat. Add the chicken drumsticks and cook, turning occasionally, for 3-4 minutes, or until sealed.

Spray the slow cooker with non stick spray.

Place the chicken drumsticks in the slow cooker and cover with vegetables and spices. Season with salt and pepper to taste, cover, and cook on low heat for 5-6 hours.

Mustard Chicken

Serves 4

Prep time: 2 min

Cooking time: 5-6 hours

Ingredients:

1 chicken, cut into 8 pieces

3 tbsp whole-grain mustard

3 tbsp low-sodium soy sauce

5 small carrots, cut in half crosswise

1 small fennel, peeled and cut into wedges

1 large red onion, cut into wedges

1 tsp dried thyme

3 tbsp extra virgin olive oil

salt and pepper, to taste

Directions:

In a bowl, combine the mustard, soy sauce, and black pepper.

Place the carrots, fennel, onion, and thyme in the slow cooker. Sprinkle with salt and olive oil and the mustard mixture.

Nestle the chicken among the vegetables, cover, and cook on low heat for 5-6 hours.

Slow Cooked Lamb with Red Wine Sauce

Serves 4

Prep time: 2 min

Cooking time: 6-7 hours

Ingredients:

4 trimmed lamb shanks

1 onion, thinly sliced

2 large carrots, roughly chopped

2-3 parsnips, roughly chopped

1 cup chicken broth

1 cup dry red wine

1 tsp brown sugar

½ tsp black pepper

½ tsp salt

Directions:

Spray the slow cooker with non stick spray.

Place the lamb shanks in it together with all other ingredients.

Cover and cook on low for 6-7 hours.

Easy Lamb and Butternut Squash Tagine

Serves 5-6

Prep time: 2 min

Cooking time: 6-8 hours

Ingredients:

2 lbs stewing lamb pieces

1 onion, finely cut

2 carrots, chopped

2 cups butternut squash, peeled, seeds removed and diced

2 garlic cloves, chopped

1 cup chicken broth

1 tbsp honey

1/4 tsp saffron threads, crushed

1/2 tsp ground ginger

½ tsp black pepper

1 tsp salt

3 tbsp extra virgin olive oil

1/2 cup chopped coriander, to serve

5 tbsp toasted pine nuts, to serve

Directions:

Spray the slow cooker with non stick spray.

Place the lamb in the slow cooker together with all other ingredients. Cover and cook on low for 6-8 hours.

Serve topped with coriander leaves and toasted pine nuts.

Lamb, Spinach and Chickpea Crock Pot

Serves 5-6

Prep time: 2 min

Cooking time: 7-9 hours

Ingredients:

2 lbs stewing lamb pieces

1 onion, finely cut

2 carrots, chopped

1 tomato, diced

2 cups spinach, chopped

1 can chickpeas, drained

1 garlic clove, chopped

1/2 cup chicken broth

1 tbsp paprika

½ tsp black pepper

½ tsp salt

3 tbsp extra virgin olive oil

Directions:

Spray the slow cooker with non stick spray.

Place the lamb in the slow cooker together with all other ingredients except the spinach.

Cover and cook on low for 7-9 hours. Add in the spinach, cover and cook on high until the spinach is wilted, about 10 minutes.

Serve with a dollop of yogurt.

Pork and Mushroom Crock Pot

Serves 4

Prep time: 2 min

Cooking time: 7-9 hours

Ingredients:

2 lbs pork tenderloin, sliced

1 lb chopped white button mushrooms

1 can cream of mushroom soup

1 cup sour cream

salt and black pepper, to taste

Directions:

Spray the slow cooker with non stick spray.

Combine all ingredients into the slow cooker.

Cover, and cook on low for 7-9 hours.

Slow Cooked Mediterranean Pork Casserole

Serves 4

Prep time: 2 min

Cooking time: 8-10 hours

Ingredients:

2 lbs pork loin, cut into cubes

1 large onion, chopped

2 cups white button mushrooms, cut

1-2 garlic cloves, finely chopped

1 green pepper,cut into strips

1 red pepper, cut into strips

1 small eggplant, peeled and diced

1 zucchini, peeled and diced

2 tomatoes, diced

1 cup chicken broth

1/2 tsp cumin

1 tbsp paprika

salt and black pepper, to taste

Directions:

Spray the slow cooker with non stick spray.

Place the pork in the slow cooker.

Add in all other ingredients and stir to combine.

Cover and cook on low 8-10 hours.

Slow Cooked Mediterranean Meatloaf

Serves 4

Prep time: 7 min

Cooking time: 6-8 hours

Ingredients:

1 lb ground beef

1 lb lb ground pork

1 small onion, chopped

1/2 cup milk

1 large loaf of bread

1-2 garlic cloves, finely chopped

2 eggs

1 tomato, diced

1/2 cup finely cut parsley

1 tsp oregano

1 tbsp paprika

½ cup grated Parmesan cheese

salt and black pepper, to taste

Directions:

Line bottom and side of slow cooker with double thickness foil; set aside.

In bowl, soak the bread loaf with milk; let stand for 10 minutes then

In large bowl, whisk the eggs. Add the tomatoes, parsley, Parmesan cheese, salt, pepper, the soaked bread, onion, garlic and oregano. Combine with a spoon. Add in veal and pork. Place in center of prepared slow cooker; shape into loaf.

Cover and cook on low 6-8 hours.

Okra and Tomato Stew

Serves: 4

Prep time: 3 min

Cooking time: 5-6 hours

Ingredients:

1-2 lb okra, trimmed

3 tomatoes, diced

3 garlic cloves, chopped

1 cup fresh parsley leaves, finely cut

3 tbsp extra virgin olive oil

1 tsp salt

black pepper, to taste

Directions:

Combine all ingredients in slow cooker. Cover and cook on low heat for 5-6 hours.

Slow Cooker Omelette with Spinach, Roasted Pepper and Feta

Serves 5-6

Prep time: 3 min

Cooking time: 2-3 hours

Ingredients:

2-3 green onions, finely chopped

5 oz baby spinach

3 roasted red peppers, diced

8 eggs, beaten

1/2 cup feta cheese, crumbled

3 tbsp milk

1 tbsp finely cut dill

black pepper, to taste

salt, to taste

Directions:

In a skillet, sauté the spinach in olive oil for 2-3 minutes or until it wilts.

Spray the slow cooker with non stick spray.

In a bowl, combine the eggs, milk, feta, dill, salt and pepper until mixed and well combined.

Add the spinach, green onions and roasted pepper to the slow cooker and stir in the egg-cheese mixture.

Cover and cook on high for 2-3 hours. Check at 2 hours if the eggs are set.

Green Beans and Potatoes

Serves: 4-4

Prep time: 2 min

Cooking time: 5-6 hours

Ingredients:

1 bag frozen green beans

3 potatoes, peeled and diced

1 tbsp tomato paste

1 carrot, sliced

1 onion, chopped

2 garlic cloves, crushed

3 tbsp extra virgin olive oil

1/2 cup fresh dill, finely chopped

½ cup water

1 tsp paprika

salt and pepper, to taste

Directions:

Combine all ingredients in slow cooker and cook on low heat for 5-6 hours. Serve warm sprinkled with fresh dill.

Cabbage and Rice Stew

Serves: 4

Prep time: 2 min

Cooking time: 5-6 hours

Ingredients:

1 cup white rice

½ medium head cabbage, cored and shredded

1 small onion, chopped

2 tomatoes, diced

2 cups vegetable broth

2 tbsp extra virgin olive oil

1 tbsp paprika

1 tsp cumin

salt, to taste

black pepper, to taste

Directions:

Combine all ingredients in slow cooker and cook on low heat for 5-6 hours.

Potato, Pea and Cauliflower Curry

Serves: 4

Prep time: 2 min

Cooking time: 5-6 hours

Ingredients:

1 lb potatoes, peeled and cubed

1 lb cauliflower, cut into small florets

1 cup fresh peas

1 onion, finely chopped

2 garlic cloves, crushed

1 cup vegetable broth

1 tsp finely grated fresh ginger

1 tbsp curry powder

2 tbsp extra virgin olive oil

1/2 cup tomato pasta sauce

1/2 cup yogurt

1 tsp cornflour

Directions:

Combine all ingredients in slow cooker and cook on low heat for 5-6 hours.

Serve with rice and extra yogurt.

Slow Cooked Mushroom, Lentil and Barley Stew

Serves 5-6

Prep time: 2 min

Cooking time: 7-8 hours

Ingredients:

2 cups button mushrooms, chopped or sliced

1 large onion, chopped

2 carrots, chopped

3/4 cup dried green lentils

1/2 cup barley

3 cups vegetable broth

1 tbsp tomato paste

1 bay leaf

1 tsp paprika

1 tsp summer savory or oregano

Directions:

Combine all ingredients in slow cooker and cook on low heat for 7-8 hours or 4-6 hours on high heat.

Rich Vegetable Stew

Serves 4-5

Prep time: 2 min

Cooking time: 8-9 hours

Ingredients:

3 potatoes, peeled and diced

2 tomatoes, diced

2 carrots, chopped

2 onions, finely chopped

1 zucchini, peeled and diced

1 eggplant, peeled and diced

1 celery rib, chopped

1 cup button mushrooms, chopped

½ cup white wine

1 bunch of parsley, finely cut

1/2 tsp black pepper

1 tsp salt

1 tsp dried basil

Combine all ingredients in slow cooker and cook on low heat for 8-9 hours or 4-6 hours on high heat.

Rice Stuffed Bell Peppers

Serves 4

Prep time: 6-7 min

Cooking time: 8-9 hours

Ingredients:

8 red bell peppers, seeded

1 cup rice, rinsed

2 cups vegetable broth

1 large onion, chopped

1 tomato, chopped

1 cup fresh parsley, chopped

2 tbsp olive oil

1 tbsp paprika

1 tsp dried basil

salt and pepper, to taste

Directions:

Heat the oil and sauté the onion for 2-3 minutes. Add in paprika, the rinsed rice, tomato, parsley and basil and season with salt and pepper to taste.

Gently stir in ½ cup of vegetable broth and cook the rice until the water is absorbed.

Stuff each pepper with the rice mixture using a spoon and arrange the peppers in a slow cooker. Add in the remaining vegetable broth.

Cover and cook on low heat for 8-9 hours or 4-6 hours on high heat.

FREE BONUS RECIPES:
20 Superfood Salad Recipes for Vibrant Health and Easy Weight Loss

Mediterranean Spinach Salad

Serves: 4

Prep time: 15 min

Ingredients:

1 bag baby spinach, washed and dried

4-5 spring onions, finely chopped

1 cucumber, peeled and cut

1/2 cup walnuts, halved and roasted

1/3 cup yogurt

2 tbsp red wine vinegar

3 tbsp extra virgin olive oil

salt and black pepper, to taste

Directions:

Whisk yogurt, olive oil and vinegar in a small bowl. Place the baby spinach leaves in a large salad bowl.

Add the onions, cucumber and walnuts. Season with black pepper and salt, stir, and toss with the dressing.

Arugula and Avocado Salad

Serves: 4

Prep time: 5 min

Ingredients:

1 bunch arugula leaves

2 avocados, peeled and sliced

1 cup strawberries, halved

1/2 cup corn kernels, cooked

1 tbsp poppy seeds

1 tbsp lemon juice

2 tbsp extra virgin olive oil

Directions:

Combine all ingredients in a salad bowl and gently toss.

Sprinkle with lemon juice and olive oil, stir, top with poppy seeds and serve.

Arugula, Radicchio and Pomegranate Salad

Serves: 4

Prep time: 5 min

Ingredients:

1 bunch arugula leaves

1 small head radicchio, chopped

1 avocado, peeled and cubed

1/2 cup pomegranate seeds, from 1 medium pomegranate

1/3 cup hazelnuts

for the dressing:

1 tbsp honey

1 tbsp balsamic vinegar

2 tbsp extra virgin olive oil

1/2 tsp salt

Directions:

Place arugula, radicchio, avocado, hazelnuts and pomegranate seeds in a large salad bowl and gently toss to combine.

Whisk dressing ingredients until smooth, pour over the salad, serve and enjoy!

Summer Green Bean Salad

Serves: 4

Prep time: 10 min

Ingredients:

1 lb trimmed green beans, cut to 2-3 inch long pieces

1 small red onion, finely cut

1 cup cherry tomatoes, halved

1 avocado, peeled, pitted and cut

3-4 garlic cloves, chopped

1 tbsp chia seeds

4 tbsp extra virgin olive oil

3/4 cup freshly grated Parmesan cheese

salt and pepper, to taste

1 cup fresh dill, finely cut, to serve

Directions:

Steam or boil the green beans for about 3-4 minutes until crisp-tender. In a colander, wash with cold water to stop cooking, then pat dry and place in a salad bowl.

Add red onion, garlic, cherry tomatoes, and avocado and sprinkle in the chia seeds. Season with lemon juice and balsamic vinegar. Toss to coat, add in the olive oil and Parmesan cheese and toss again. Season to taste with salt and freshly ground black pepper.

Refrigerate for an hour and serve sprinkled with fresh dill.

Three Bean Salad

Serves: 4

Prep time: 15 min

Ingredients:

½ cup canned chickpeas, drained and rinsed

½ cup canned kidney beans, drained and rinsed

1 lb trimmed green beans, cut to 2-3 inch long pieces

a bunch of radishes, sliced

5-6 green onions, chopped

½ cup cilantro leaves, finely cut

for the dressing:

2 tbsp honey

½ tsp ground dry mustard

1 tsp garlic powder

3 tbsp extra virgin olive oil

1/3 cup apple cider vinegar

Directions:

Steam or boil the green beans for about 3-4 minutes until crisp-tender. In a colander, wash with cold water to stop cooking, pat dry and place in a salad bowl. Mix in the chickpeas, kidney beans, green onions, radishes and cilantro leaves.

In a smaller bowl, whisk together the apple cider vinegar, olive oil, honey, mustard, garlic powder, black pepper and salt. Pour over the salad and toss gently to coat.

Cover, refrigerate for at least 1 hour, toss again and serve.

Beet and Bean Sprout Salad

Serves: 4

Prep time: 10 min

Ingredients:

5-6 beet greens, finely cut

2 tomatoes, sliced

1 cup bean sprouts, washed

1/2 cup pine nuts

for the dressing:

2 garlic cloves, crushed

4 tbsp lemon juice

4 tbsp extra virgin olive oil

1 tsp salt

Directions:

Place pine nuts in a small fry pan over medium heat and cook for 2 minutes, stirring regularly, or until golden. Remove from heat and set aside.

In a large salad bowl toss together beet greens, bean sprouts and tomatoes. Whisk the olive oil, lemon juice, salt and garlic and pour it over the salad.

Sprinkle with pine nuts, and serve chilled.

Beet Salad with Walnuts

Serves: 4

Prep time: 25 min

Ingredients:

3 medium beets, steamed and diced

1 red onion, sliced

1/2 cup walnuts, halved

1 tbsp lemon juice

2 tbsp olive oil

4-5 mint leaves

½ tsp salt

Directions:

Wash the beets, trim the stems, and steam them over boiling water until cooked through. Plunge the beets in cold water, and peel when they are cool enough to handle.

Dice the beets and place them in a salad bowl. Add in walnuts, onion, lemon juice and olive oil and toss to combine.

Chill, and serve sprinkled with fresh mint leaves.

Beet Salad with Yogurt

Serves: 4

Prep time: 25 min

Ingredients:

4 medium beets, steamed and cubed

1 cup strained yogurt

2 garlic cloves, crushed

1 tsp lemon juice

2 tbsp olive oil

1/2 tsp dried mint

½ tsp salt

Directions:

Wash the beets, trim the stems, and steam them over boiling water until cooked through. Rinse the beets with cold water, and peel when they are cool enough to handle. Peel and pat dry with a paper towel. Cut the beets in small cubes and place them in a deep salad bowl.

Whisk the yogurt with garlic, mint, olive oil and lemon juice in a small bowl. Pour over other ingredients and toss to combine. Serve cold.

Warm Beet and Lentil Salad

Serves: 5-6

Prep time: 10 min

Ingredients:

1 14 oz can brown lentils, drained, rinsed

1 14 oz can sliced pickled beets, drained

1 cup baby arugula leaves

1 small red onion, chopped

2 garlic cloves, crushed

6 oz feta cheese, crumbled

1 tbsp extra virgin olive oil

for the dressing

3 tbsp extra virgin olive oil

1 tbsp red wine vinegar

1 tsp summer savory

salt and black pepper, to taste

Directions:

Heat one tablespoon of olive oil in a frying pan and gently sauté onion for 2-3 minutes or until softened. Add in garlic, lentils and beets. Cook, stirring, for 2 minutes.

Whisk together remaining olive oil, vinegar, summer savory, salt and pepper. Add to the lentils and toss to coat. Combine baby arugula, feta and lentil mixture in a bowl. Toss gently to combine and serve.

Roasted Vegetable Salad

Serves: 4-5

Prep time: 30 min

Ingredients:

3 tomatoes, halved

1 zucchini, quartered

1 fennel bulb, thinly sliced

2 small eggplants, ends trimmed, quartered

1 large red pepper, halved, deseeded, cut into strips

2 medium onions, quartered

1 tsp oregano

2 tbsp extra virgin olive oil

for the dressing

2/3 cup yogurt

1 tbsp fresh lemon juice

1 small garlic clove, chopped

Directions:

Place the zucchini, eggplant, pepper, fennel, onions, tomatoes and olive oil on a lined baking sheet. Season with salt, pepper and oregano and roast in a 500 degrees F oven until golden, about 20 minutes.

Whisk the yogurt, lemon juice and garlic in a bowl. Taste and season with salt and pepper. Divide the vegetables in 4-5 plates. Top with the yogurt mixture and serve.

Warm Leek and Sweet Potato Salad

Serves 4-5

Prep time: 30 min

Ingredients:

1.5 lb sweet potato, unpeeled, cut into 1 inch pieces

4 small leeks, trimmed and cut into 1 inch slices

5-6 white mushrooms, halved

1 cup baby arugula leaves

2 tbsp extra virgin olive oil

for the dressing

½ cup yogurt

1 tbsp Dijon mustard

Directions:

Preheat oven to 350 F. Line a baking tray with baking paper. Place the sweet potato, leeks and mushrooms on the baking tray. Drizzle with olive oil and toss to coat. Roast for 20 minutes or until golden.

Combine yogurt and mustard in a small bowl or cup. Place vegetables, mushrooms and baby arugula in a salad bowl and toss to combine. Serve drizzled with the yogurt mixture.

Mediterranean Avocado Salad

Serves: 5-6

Prep time: 10 min

Ingredients:

2 avocados, peeled, halved and cut into cubes

½ ciabatta roll, cut into small cubes

2 cups cherry tomatoes, halved

½ red onion, thinly sliced

1 large cucumber, halved, sliced

½ cup green olives, pitted, halved

½ cup black olives, pitted, sliced

6 oz feta cheese, cut into cubes

7-8 fresh basil leaves, torn

½ cup parsley leaves, finely cut

4 tbsp extra virgin olive oil

3 tbsp red wine vinegar

Directions:

Line a baking tray with baking paper and place ciabatta cubes. Drizzle with one tablespoon of olive oil. Season with salt and pepper and gently toss to coat. Cook under the grill for 2-3 minutes or until golden. Set aside to cool.

Place all vegetables, feta, basil, olives, and ciabatta cubes in a large salad bowl. Gently toss to combine then sprinkle with vinegar and remaining olive oil. Season with salt and pepper and gently toss again. Sprinkle with parsley and serve.

Easy Artichoke and Bean Salad

Serves: 5-6

Prep time: 15 min

Ingredients:

1 14 oz can white beans, drained

2-3 large handfuls podded broad beans

3 marinated artichoke hearts, quartered

for the dressing:

2 tbsp extra virgin olive oil

1 tbsp lemon juice

1 tbsp apple cider vinegar

1 tbsp fresh mint, chopped

salt and pepper, to taste

Directions:

Cook the broad beans in boiling, unsalted water for 2-3 minutes or until tender. Drain and refresh under running cold water. Combine with the white beans and quartered marinated artichoke hearts in a large salad bowl.

In a smaller bowl, whisk olive oil, lemon juice, vinegar and mint. Pour over the bean mixture. Season with salt and pepper and toss gently to combine.

Artichoke, Mushroom and Tomato Salad

Serves: 4-5

Prep time: 15 min

Ingredients:

1 14 oz can artichoke hearts, drained, cut quartered

7-8 white mushrooms, halved

½ cup sun-dried tomatoes, halved

½ cup walnuts, halved and toasted

1 bag baby arugula leaves

2 tbsp lemon juice

1 tbsp extra virgin olive oil

salt and pepper, to taste

Directions:

Place the artichokes, mushrooms, walnuts and tomatoes in a large bowl and set aside for 5-6 minutes.

Whisk the lemon juice and olive oil in a small bowl until smooth.

Add the baby arugula leaves to the artichoke mixture. Drizzle with dressing, season with salt and pepper and toss gently before serving.

Avocado and Cucumber Salad

Serves: 4-5

Prep time: 10 min

Ingredients:

2 avocados, peeled, halved and sliced

½ red onion, thinly sliced

1 large cucumber, halved, sliced

½ radicchio, trimmed, finely shredded

7-8 fresh basil leaves, torn

for the dressing:

1 tbsp black olive paste

2 tbsp extra virgin olive oil

1 tbsp red balsamic vinegar

1 tbsp lemon juice

salt and pepper, to taste

Directions:

Combine avocado, radicchio and cucumber in a bowl. Place vinegar, oil, lemon juice and black olive paste in a small bowl and whisk until very well combined.

Pour over the salad, season with salt and pepper and toss gently to combine.

Easy Vitamin Salad

Serves: 4-5

Prep time: 10 min

Ingredients:

6 small new potatoes

1 carrot, peeled and cut

7 oz cauliflower, cut into florets

7 oz baby Brussels sprouts, trimmed

3-4 broccoli florets

for the dressing:

3 tbsp fresh lemon juice

2 tbsp extra virgin olive oil

2 garlic cloves, crushed

Directions:

Cook potatoes in a steamer basket over boiling water for 10 minutes or until just tender. Add in the cauliflower, broccoli and Brussels sprouts and cook for 5 minutes more. Using a vegetable peeler, cut thin ribbons from carrot. Add to the steam basket and cook for 4 minutes more. Refresh under cold running water and set aside for to cool.

Whisk the lemon juice, oil, and garlic in a small bowl. Season with salt and pepper.

Cut the potatoes in half lengthwise and place them in a salad bowl. Add in cauliflower, Brussels sprouts, carrot and broccoli. Pour the dressing over the salad and gently toss to combine.

Rainbow Superfood Salad

Serves: 4-5

Prep time: 10 min

Ingredients:

2 cups shredded red cabbage

1 cup broccoli or sunflower sprouts

1 medium cucumber

1 red apple

1 carrot, peeled

for the dressing:

1 tbsp red wine vinegar

2 tbsp extra virgin olive oil

1 tsp sumac

salt and pepper, to taste

Directions:

Using a vegetable peeler, cut thin ribbons from carrot, cucumber and apple. Place in a large bowl. Add cabbage and sprouts. Whisk ingredients for the dressing until smooth. Pour over salad, toss to combine and serve.

Cabbage, Carrots and Turnip Salad

Serves: 4

Prep time: 15 min

Ingredients:

7 oz white cabbage, shredded

7 oz carrots, shredded

5 oz white turnips, shredded

1 tbsp sesame seeds

½ a bunch of dill

2 tbsp white vinegar

2 tbsp extra virgin olive oil

salt and black pepper, to taste

Directions:

Combine first three ingredients in a large salad bowl. Add in sesame seeds, salt, vinegar and olive oil.

Stir and sprinkle with dill. Set aside for 5 minutes, stir again and serve.

Spicy Carrot Salad

Serves: 4

Prep time: 10 min

Ingredients:

4 carrots, shredded

1 apple, peeled, cored and shredded

2 garlic cloves, crushed

1/2 cup fresh dill, very finely cut

1 tbsp sesame seeds

2 tbsp lemon juice

1 tbsp honey

1/2 tsp cumin

1/2 tsp grated ginger

salt and pepper, to taste

Directions:

Combine all ingredients in a deep salad bowl.

Toss to combine, chill for 30 minutes, top with sesame seeds and serve.

Warm Tomato Salad

Serves: 4-5

Prep time: 10 min

Ingredients:

4 tomatoes, sliced

1 cup cherry tomatoes, halved

½ small red onion, very finely cut

2 garlic cloves, crushed

1 tbsp dried mint

2 tbsp extra virgin olive oil

1 tbsp balsamic vinegar

Directions:

Gently heat oil in a non-stick frying pan over low heat. Cook garlic and tomatoes, stirring occasionally, for 4-5 minutes or until tomatoes are warm but firm.

Remove from heat and place in a plate. Add in red onion, vinegar and dried mint. Season with salt and pepper to taste and serve.

About the Author

Alissa Grey is a fitness and nutrition enthusiast who loves to teach people about losing weight and feeling better about themselves. She lives in a small French village in the foothills of a beautiful mountain range with her husband, three teenage kids, two free spirited dogs, and various other animals.

Alissa is incredibly lucky to be able to cook and eat natural foods, mostly grown nearby, something she's done since she was a teenager. She enjoys yoga, running, reading, hanging out with her family, and growing organic vegetables and herbs.

21036727R00050

Printed in Great Britain
by Amazon